# Chipmunk Facts: Chipmunks
# A Picture Book for Kids About Chipmunks
### By Lisa Strattin
### © 2013 Lisa Strattin
### Revised © 2020

# 8 BOOK BOX SET

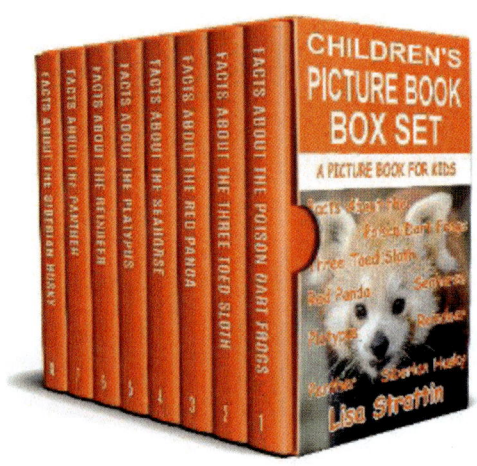

- **FACTS ABOUT THE POISON DART FROGS**
- **FACTS ABOUT THE THREE TOED SLOTH**
- **FACTS ABOUT THE RED PANDA**
- **FACTS ABOUT THE SEAHORSE**
- **FACTS ABOUT THE PLATYPUS**
- **FACTS ABOUT THE REINDEER**
- **FACTS ABOUT THE PANTHER**
- **FACTS ABOUT THE SIBERIAN HUSKY**

LisaStrattin.com/BookBundle

**Facts for Kids Picture Books by Lisa Strattin**

**Pygmy Rabbit, Vol 153**

**Jumping Rabbit, Vol 154**

**Mini Rabbits, Vol 155**

**Blue Quail, Vol 156**

**Mountain Quail, Vol 157**

**Quokka, Vol 158**

**Quoll, Vol 159**

**Raccoon, Vol 160**

**Raccoon Dog, Vol 161**

**Radiated Tortoise, Vol 162**

**Sign Up for New Release Emails Here**

**http://LisaStrattin.com/subscribe-here**

All rights reserved. No part of this book may be reproduced by any means whatsoever without the written permission from the author, except brief portions quoted for purpose of review.

All information in this book has been carefully researched and checked for factual accuracy. However, the author and publisher makes no warranty, express or implied, that the information contained herein is appropriate for every individual, situation or purpose and assume no responsibility for errors or omissions. The reader assumes the risk and full responsibility for all actions, and the author will not be held responsible for any loss or damage, whether consequential, incidental, special or otherwise, that may result from the information presented in this book.

All images are purchased from stock photo sites or royalty free for commercial use.

I have relied on my own observations as well as many different sources for this book and I have done my best to check facts and give credit where it is due. In the event that any material is used without proper permission, please contact me so that the oversight can be corrected.

**★★COVER IMAGE★★**

https://www.flickr.com/photos/tamasrepus/35525969040/

**★★ADDITIONAL IMAGES★★**

https://www.flickr.com/photos/157901423@N06/42482566720/

https://www.flickr.com/photos/phrawr/13913758237/

https://www.flickr.com/photos/alvaroreguly/24468299305/

https://www.flickr.com/photos/monkeypuzzle/6067234332/

https://www.flickr.com/photos/25036726@N07/17986336423/

https://www.flickr.com/photos/tmwolf/3898227506/

https://www.flickr.com/photos/robbie1/30362162631/

https://www.flickr.com/photos/sadiehart/7612975186/

https://www.flickr.com/photos/photographybycolby/10377437484/

https://www.flickr.com/photos/nstawski/7944130350/

https://www.flickr.com/photos/10233916@N03/4771833141/

https://www.flickr.com/photos/carolineccb/7407706186/

Contents

APPEARANCE ................................................................. 9

SIZE ............................................................................... 13

LIFE SPAN/HABITAT .................................................... 15

DIET .............................................................................. 19

CHILDREN .................................................................... 29

## APPEARANCE

There are 50 species of chipmunk, which are part of the rodent family. As a close relative of the squirrel they have slight differences in their appearance, but they usually are brown, reddish-orange or grey in color with stripes running along their sides and back.

Their bushy tail is nearly always white underneath it as is their belly. Their dark eyes are on the sides of their faces.

Their ears are very small but they have acute hearing that alerts them to predators. They are obsessed with cleanliness and that is why you'll see them cleaning themselves when not eating or searching for food.

## SIZE

The average chipmunk, depending on what type of chipmunk it is, usually is between 7.5 and 11 inches long. They normally weigh between 1.1 to 4.4 ounces. The tail itself is about 3 to 5 inches long.

## LIFE SPAN/HABITAT

Nearly all chipmunk species live in North America, and they can even be found as far south as Mexico. You'll find them in deserts, valleys, and northern forests. The northern forests where alpine and sequoia trees provide them with plenty of protection seem to be their favorite spots.

One of the most common, yet surprising places they live are in flower and tree beds that are surrounded by small brick walls created by people. Since North America has the kinds of trees they love to live in, it's a perfect spot for them They live for 2 or 7 years, on average.

If they aren't in the trees they might build burrows down in the ground, using leaves they gather as a bed.

## DIET

Chipmunks like to find their food just about anywhere, but they usually look for food where they can hide easily. Given their speed at escaping, they usually look in places like logs, rocks, trees and flower beds.

Since they go to bed as the sun goes down and come up right before the sun rises, they are hunting food nearly all day, resting for only a few hours a day, when they need a nap. They use both paws to eat their food, which they usually nibble on.

For the most part, chipmunks are omnivores, meaning they eat both plants and meat. But the only thing it eats that is considered meat would be insects, small frogs, worms and birds' eggs. Their mouths can expand almost as much as the size of their head if they need to store food while they are gathering it up.

Some chipmunks have been known to hold as many as nine or ten nuts in their mouth!

Since their teeth are constantly growing, if they lose or chip a tooth, another will grow back in its place. This is great for when they have to hunt for food.

They usually go for food that they can easily grab, like nuts, berries and fruit. Sometimes they will eat seeds too, but only as a last resort. They are particularly fond of acorns and hazel nuts.

Chipmunks like to live in trees or burrows. These are a great home for them to hibernate during the winter because it provides warmth. They also store their nuts, berries, and fruit inside these burrows and trees.

Think of a tree as not only their home, but as their refrigerator or pantry, as well.

Now it should be remembered that chipmunks, like squirrels, tend to be friendly to people. They don't usually make it a habit of taking food from people, but when they do, it's a snack for them.

## CHILDREN

Chipmunks are some of the most sociable of animals, but they don't socialize with other chipmunks unless it is absolutely necessary. They just find themselves in a difficult situation because once winter comes around, they can and will, if necessary, protect the food they are searching for and storing.

It is a lot of fun to watch them, but children should not try to catch them.

They make a chirping sound which alerts them to females who want to mate with them in the Spring. These sounds can also be used to warn other chipmunks of dangerous predators that are nearby. They also shake their tail if they sense that a predator is close.

Chipmunks are fun to watch. Don't forget that even though they are cute – **they are not usually pets**. Don't try to pick one up, you might scare them. But enjoy watching them play and look for nuts.

Please leave me a review here:

http://lisastrattin.com/Review-Vol-5

For more Kindle Downloads Visit **Lisa Strattin Author Page** on Amazon Author Central

http://amazon.com/author/lisastrattin

To see upcoming titles, visit my website at **LisaStrattin.com**– all books available on kindle!

http://lisastrattin.com

# FREE EBOOK

## FACTS ABOUT THE SKUNK

### A PICTURE BOOK FOR KIDS

*Lisa Strattin*

LisaStrattin.com/Sign-Up

Made in the USA
Middletown, DE
02 August 2023

36138271R10020